AF824157

WELCOME FROM

James M. Tolles, *Editor*

Bud Donahue, *Illustrator*

Monica Maccaux, *Graphic Designer*

Bruce Leslie, *Contributing Editor*

We each have The Choice—
We can work for Money—
Or we can make Money work for Us.

ISBN 978-0-692-07565-4

© 2018 Conrad Leslie, All rights reserved.

This information is being published to offer guidance for arriving at sound financial market decisions by new investors and traders. The material contained herein is considered reliable but is not guaranteed as to its accuracy, application or completeness. Also it should not be construed as a suggestion to buy or sell any securities or commodities.

30 TIPS FOR
BETTER INVESTING

BY CONRAD LESLIE

"Successful speculation is anything but a mere guess. To be consistently successful, an investor or speculator must have rules to guide him."

- Jesse L. Livermore

AT THE BEGINNING

It is presently fashionable in some circles of America to have as an objective—the making of things average. Let me start by stating that I am opposed to anyone becoming an average President, member of Congress, student, professor, teacher, businessman, doctor or lawyer.

I am also opposed to anyone becoming an average musician, football or baseball player, newspaper reporter, farmer, mayor, or trader or investor in America's financial markets.

I am opposed to anyone being restricted to an average income, average education, average home, average automobile, or to the production of average cattle or the growing of an average crop of wheat, corn or soybeans.

We live in an economic system that is creative, stimulating, dynamic, ever changing, exciting and challenging. It offers profits and losses and the freedom of choice for the investment of your money. In America's society, as demands change and supplies adjust-prices go up and prices go down and such create gain opportunities for each of us.

RULES

TABLE OF CONTENTS

TIP NO. ONE

#1

BE BOLD, ALWAYS BE BOLD, ABOVE ALL BE BOLD!

ONE

When a conclusion is obvious to all of the public and your analysis disputes the obvious, remember that when the final period arrives, the viewpoint of the majority can often prove to be incorrect. If the present thinking has been in vogue for some time and is becoming stale, at the sign of positive weakness in the obvious, as evidenced by a stumbling in the price patterns, move boldly and with strength, especially if you believe your conclusion will prevail.

"Beware of the obvious."

Successful traders are mentally alert to leave the thinking of the crowd, especially after a long and extended period, and when new price action gives some evidence of weakness in the obvious through changes in patterns of the price trend.

Semper Bold

TIP NO.

#2

DO NOT TRY TO BUY AT THE BOTTOM AND SELL AT THE TOP

TWO

This can't be done consistently—except by dreamers.

Try to buy when a major price move is getting underway, and try to sell when the price action indicates the move may have exhausted itself.

Be content to watch your competitors strive for the privilege of announcing that they were able to buy at the bottom and sell at the top. The results of habitual attempts at such a practice will usually cancel out early successes. This is because the sweet taste of temporary perfection often results in an increase in recklessness, when one finds that he has fallen out of that unusual achievement category.

Extreme prices last for only a few moments and are seldom realized by more than a few.

B
S
S
B

TIP NO.

#3

ALWAYS BUY AND SELL "AT THE MARKET"

THREE

There is no successful "cut rate" approach to buying and selling securities or commodities. More money has been lost by trying to save a tenth of a point and through indecisive orders than has ever been gained. Unless you use up-to-date charts for guidance as to specific points for buy or sell orders via stop-loss orders, always enter "at the market" buying and selling orders.

Your primary objective should be to buy into situations where the momentum is such as to carry the price in your favor beyond your commitment level. Avoid the practice of trying to buy during so called "healthy reactions" with under lying price limit orders.

SOLD OUT
SALE
HURRY! HURRY!

TIP NO.

#4

BUY IN ANTICIPATION AND SELL ON REALIZATION

FOUR

Increased earnings reports, stock-split announcements, dividend increases, corporate buy outs, production estimates and other important statistical reports have a way of being discounted beforehand by the market. Buy in anticipation of such announcements, but be prepared to take profits when they become a matter of record.

Often it will prove valuable to review the trading volume during the recent sessions prior to an important statistical announcement. If it has been unusually heavy, then remain alert to liquidate at the first sign of weakness. It is probable that the market may have already discounted the situation through the early actions of those who have had the development under close study.

The test of any new development from the standpoint of price strength is the following:

1. How did the market close on the day the announcement became public?
2. How did the market close on the following day when the announcement appeared in the newspapers read by the public?
3. How did the market close on the third day when everyone knew the news?

TIP NO.

#5

NEVER SEND GOOD MONEY AFTER BAD

FIVE

Do not average down in a situation that has turned sour, and do not put up more margin money. When the price has gone against you to or beyond a reasonable stop-loss point, close out the position. Then look for a situation where the price action is going in the same direction as your judgment tells you it should. The market will tell a speculator when he or she is wrong.

Should you have several positions in the market and receive a maintenance margin call, liquidate those with the largest losses and retain those positions which have developed profits.

A most important rule to remember about trading or investing is that you must preserve your capital.

TIP NO.

#6

BEWARE OF TOO MUCH COMPANY

SIX

It is usually well to be with the stream of public sentiment. However, when you sense your position is becoming crowded by the support of "eleventh-hour bulls" and too many "followers," be mentally alert to liquidate and stand aside when price patterns develop positive signs of a price-trend exhaustion.

The entire expectations of the majority seldom become completed facts, especially those, which develop late in the period when enthusiasm nears its peak.

Public excitement is often the greatest at tops and bottoms. This can be demonstrated through short-lived, final, extreme price moves.

When everyone is thinking alike, no one is thinking very much.

TIP NO.

#7

WHEN YOU DO NOT KNOW WHAT TO DO, CONSIDER DOING NOTHING

SEVEN

Strive for the positive approach. When a situation appears to be in balance, or a friend has advised you to buy or sell and you are still undecided, do nothing. Be patient. Weigh the pros and cons until your mind moves your mental scale toward the dominate weight of either confidence or doubt.

A very successful futures trader has observed "A great deal of the time, I'm in a quandary not knowing what to do because the facts seem so conflicting.

At such periods, I'm better off not trading at all."

You are not forced to play every hand. Learn to wait until the market comes to you on your own terms.

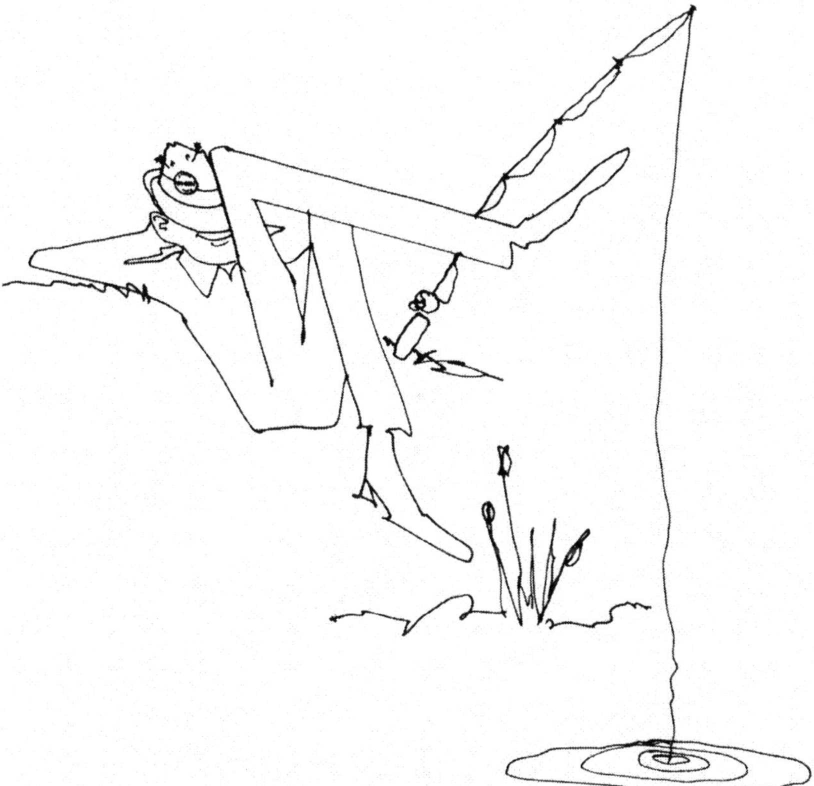

TIP NO.

#8

DO NOT EXPECT TO BE RIGHT ALL OF THE TIME

EIGHT

Six or seven successes out of ten attempts are an excellent average. Some successful traders profit only four out of ten attempts. They are successful because early in life they learned the primary rule of taking small losses and letting profits accrue.

Most successful traders recognize that market conditions change. An original commitment may have been correct at the time it was initiated. However, one must be prepared to acknowledge that later events can and may change the outlook. To accept these happenings as routine, and with graciousness, is to achieve maturity.

TIP NO.

#9

ALWAYS SPECULATE AS IF YOU DO NOT HAVE MONEY TO LOSE

NINE

A casual trader seldom arrives at the halls of success. Every market decision should be treated with intensity and weighed as though it were the most important of your career.

Never allow the accumulation of profits to result in a sloppy trading technique. Once such a habit is acquired, it is difficult to break and will usually be carried over into those periods when profit possibilities are poor and good technique is a necessity for survival.

TIP NO.

#10

KEEP A CASH RESERVE TO TAKE ADVANTAGE OF THOSE UNEXPECTED OPPORTUNITIES

TEN

Many traders prefer to remain fully invested rather than retain some cash reserve.

This approach can act as a handicap. It may result in the establishment of several commitments about which one does not have strong convictions. Strong convictions regarding each commitment are one of the requirements for success.

No trader can foresee all of the good profit possibilities the near future will unfold. The world's economic and scientific discovery fields are in a constant state of change. This is true also of a trader's sources of new information.

Stocks in the marketplace are continually shifting their colors from red to green and from green to red. At times, there are more greens than reds and at other times more reds than greens. Occasionally even the brightness of color may become obscured by fog or haze.

It is good practice to retain some funds for those outstanding and unexpected situations, which occasionally occur two or three times a year.

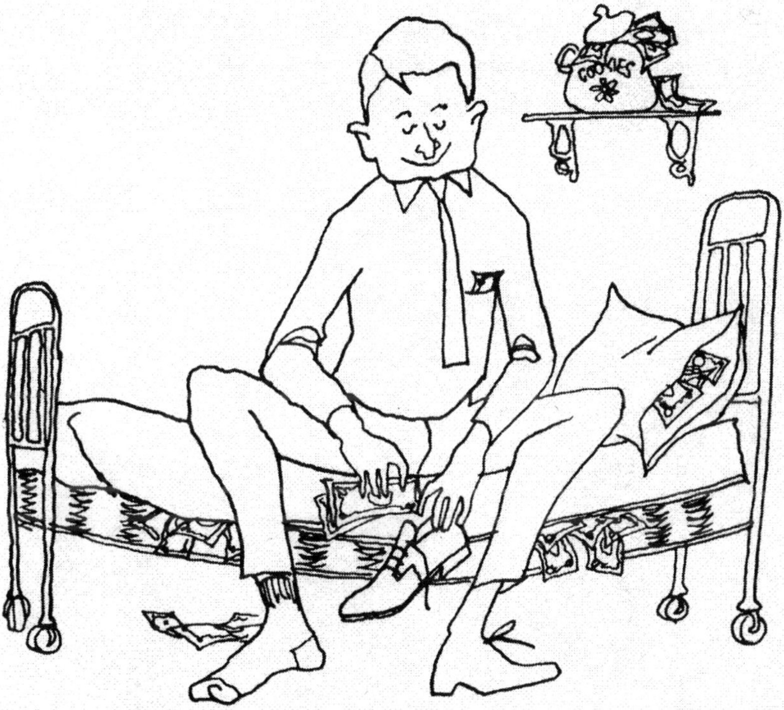
COOKIES

TIP NO.

#11

IT TAKES THE ROAR OF A LION TO MOVE PRICES UP BUT THE SQUEAK OF A MOUSE TO MOVE PRICES DOWN

ELEVEN

It generally takes a great deal of fanfare and publicity to create confidence and attract the public into exchanging dollars for stocks or futures contracts. Some important development is usually required to get a good upward price move underway.

On the other hand, the average person tends towards pessimism. It doesn't take much to lower one's confidence to a point where one will liquidate in order to turn profits or loses into safer dollars.

Bull markets are usually slow and of longer duration as traders try to develop positions for long term capital gains.

Bear markets are usually of sharp and shorter duration. Few traders sell short, therefore there is less underlying buying support to absorb and slow the decline.

Also, margin calls can force the longs unexpectedly to sell out over extended positions.

TIP NO.

#12

STRIVE TO THINK AS A CYNIC

TWELVE

To become a successful trader, you must train yourself to question everything. Then, only believe the proof of the pudding, that what the action of the market confirms.

The utmost caution is warranted if you are long and the price does not go up when there is new bullish news. Or, if you are short and the price does not continue to sell off on new bearish reports.

Be careful to become neither a pessimist nor an optimist, only a habitual neutral with an open but questioning mind.

"Stocks are sometimes the strongest when they look the weakest, and weakest when they look the strongest."

One should be ready to become contrary at times, but not obstinate. Successful traders usually learn early in their careers that it often pays to "Beware of the obvious."

TIP NO.

#13

NEVER BUY UNLESS YOU ARE FIRMLY CONVINCED YOU WILL BE ABLE TO SELL OUT AT A HIGHER PRICE. NEVER SELL SHORT UNLESS YOU ARE CONVINCED THAT YOU WILL BE ABLE TO BUY BACK AT A LOWER PRICE.

THIRTEEN

Do not make a commitment merely to keep your funds working, or to earn the current dividend. Stock values are constantly changing. Because price appreciation is your first objective, be patient and extremely selective before committing your funds to the marketplace.

Do not make a commitment in the market unless you sense that your thinking is ahead of that of some and preferably most of the crowd. To succeed as a trader, you must do a better job at forecasting values than the current market is doing.

SEASONAL
SAVINGS

TIP NO.

#14

ALWAYS ACCEPT AN UNEXPECTED QUICK PROFIT

FOURTEEN

There will be times when you discover that the market has unexpectedly presented you with a sizable profit within a few days after the commitment was initiated. Often these fast profits will prove to be short-lived and the market will pull back to the level of your original commitment- to build a base for a long-term advance.

Be prepared mentally, on the first sign of weakness, to bank a surprising and extreme quick profit. Especially, if the move can be identified as a temporary news or an advisory pronouncement rather than a basic change in long-term fundamentals.

A quick bird in the hand today can be worth three in the bush of tomorrow. There will be times, during an interim workout period, when the total market's down pressure becomes greater than the quick strength "special situation." Three out of four stocks will move with the total up or down or sidewise market's momentum direction.

TIP NO.

#15

WHEN IN DOUBT, REDUCE THE POSITION

FIFTEEN

Successful trading requires a positive approach to the market. Know why you have made a commitment at all times. Start to liquidate when developments arise which result in you beginning to question the wisdom of the original decision. Continue to liquidate as long as you are disturbed.

Initiate a trade to the long side on "Yes, it's good," or to the short side on "No, it's bad." Retain a conservative approach as long as the answer appears to be one of "Maybe it's good, or maybe it's bad."

Pareto, the great Italian sociologist, observed that the distinguishing characteristic of the speculative type person is that he is constantly preoccupied with the possibilities of new conditions.

TIP NO.

#16

LEARN TO THINK FOR YOURSELF

SIXTEEN

Decisions arrived at by committees or groups of people often reflect the influence of the dominant "popular" personality.

Decisions can also be determined by the worst opinion of the weakest thinker in the group.

The strength of a chain of decisions will be influenced by its weakest links.

Learn to stand straight and tall and on your own two feet. Learn to think for yourself.

UPTOWN
EXPRESS

TIP NO.

#17

DECISIONS MADE UNDER PRESSURE ARE USUALLY WRONG

SEVENTEEN

Poor decisions can develop when outside pressures, which have no direct bearing on the commitment, come to the front. Such situations can develop when a trader has an overextended market position and a requirement for immediate funds arises. Sickness, divorce, a recent death, a change in job or income, all can create temporary stress and unusual mental fatigue.

Do not attempt to make important market decisions when your mind is not fully able to concentrate in a normal manner.

TIP NO.

#18

RUN PROMPTLY AT THE FIRST APPROACH OF POSITIVE DANGER

EIGHTEEN

Be prepared to liquidate your position quickly at the first sign of clearly adverse market news which is not in keeping with your expectations. An unexpectedly poor earnings report, a dividend reduction, a negative Food and Drug decision (stocks) or a surprise U.S.D.A. crop production estimate (futures) are examples.

"The first price is usually the best price."

Leave the theater when you first smell smoke. Don't wait for the fire to break out. Especially when the presence of considerable smoke is verified by important changes in price patterns.

"Success rides on the hour of decision."

TIP NO.

#19

MAJOR PRICE MOVES USUALLY CARRY FURTHER THAN STATISTICS SEEM TO JUSTIFY

NINETEEN

Major price moves, which have attracted a great deal of attention generally overshoot a logical price end.

Be prepared to remain with a major move beyond a forecasted price level.

Await evidence from the price of the exhaustion of a trend. Then be bold.

"Whatever traders do—they tend to overdo."

TIP NO.

#20

BE PREPARED FOR SUDDEN AND DRASTIC SUCCESS AND FAILURES

TWENTY

Train yourself to make rather fast and positive decisions regarding the issuance of orders, once the issue is clear, irrespective of your profit or loss. This is done in order to take advantage of existing situations before deterioration occurs. Markets and prices move rapidly and are in a continual state of flux. They respond readily to major new developments, which will result in shifts in public opinion. Today's lack of action in regard an existing position, when a fundamental issue has suddenly become clearly resolved, can often become tomorrow's regret.

Learn to keep your cool and remain relaxed. After a thorough review of the profit or loss in the trade just liquidated yesterday, learn from the experience. Do not brood about the new news relative to yesterday's trade that developed shortly thereafter.

A successful trader keeps his or her eyes on the ball and walks away from those irritations and exasperations, which can exert a detrimental influence on his or her total mental attitude.

Think success, resolutely and persistently.

TIP NO.

#21

DO NOT TRADE MONEY, TRADE PRICE MOVES

TWENTY-ONE

Some traders have the habit of arriving at a conclusion as to how much money they would like to take out of a price move. Often this decision is unconsciously motivated by desire rather than market logic.

Thoughts of a dollar profit objective can overpower market judgment and result in a failure to recognize the development of a critical reversal point, which may develop just short of a dollar-profit objective. Do not handicap your thinking by counting up the number of dollars you expect to take out of a particular situation. Stay with commitment as long as it is sound, and liquidate it when it turns bad. Then, and only then, add up the dollar profits.

Even the most successful professional traders and financiers are unable to predict how, where, or when a trade will end.

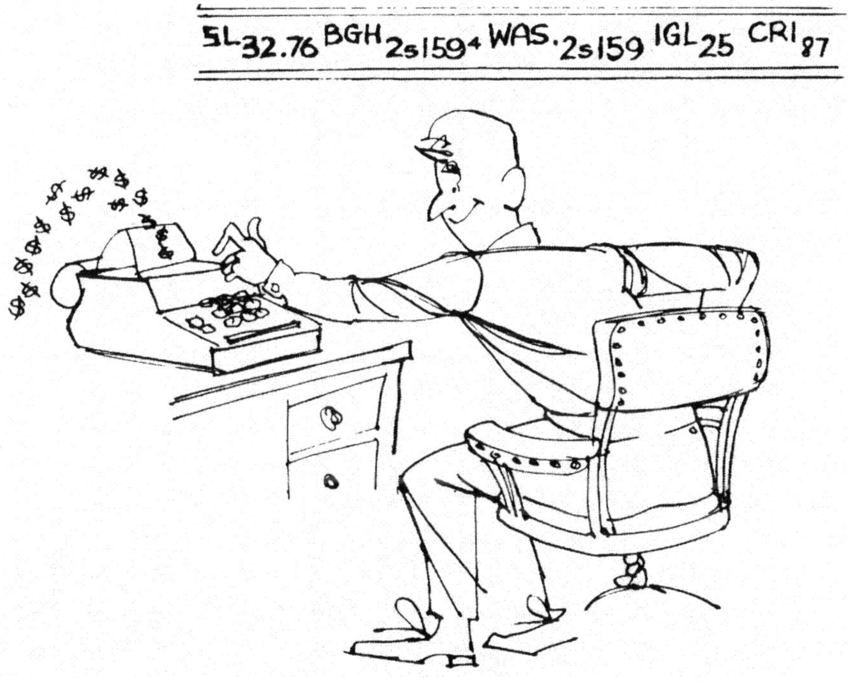

SL 32.76 BGH 2s159 4 WAS. 2s159 IGL 25 CRI 87

TIP NO.

#22

IT IS BETTER TO LOSE YOUR OPINION RATHER THAN YOUR MONEY

TWENTY-TWO

When the price action and your opinion do not coincide, stand aside until they are in harmony. Many a trader has ultimately been proven right and yet lost his capital during the period required for incubation. Especially, if the trader believes he or she is a super analyst and too early assumes the weakness of a position, which reflects an over concentration on the distant future and not enough on the present.

When developing a position in the market, be prepared to wait and move in concert with signals by the price that the situation is starting to come around to your point of view.

Opinions are of little value to a speculator unless and until the market acts accordingly.

TIP NO.

#23

THE ELEMENT OF CHANCE SHOULD NOT BE OVERLOOKED WHEN ESTABLISHING A MARKET POSITION

TWENTY-THREE

Certain events will occur such as terrorist attacks, sudden wars, explosions, fires, rains, riots, revolutions, wrecks, presidential illnesses, etc. which cannot be predicted. Never put yourself in a position where an unexpected development of this type catches you with an overextended position.

Should you find yourself trapped by a market that is reacting to a major development, remember that fear is usually a temporary emotion stemming from an unknown that appears harmful. When fear overrules reason, the impulse is to sell.

The lowest prices during a break induced by fright in the market are always reached just before the unknown becomes more identifiable.

Keep in mind the fact that major unexpected news can develop over weekends.

FORMULA
27
SECRET
NEW CITY
CHEMICAL CO.

TIP NO.

#24

REMEMBER THAT MAJOR PRICE MOVES OFTEN LEAP TO CONCLUSIONS

TWENTY-FOUR

After a long and sustained price move, be alert for a sizable price gap on the morning opening from the previous day's close—as a sign that the end might be near.

An "exhaustion gap" usually will not be filled by a price decline to below the previous close until late in the market session. This development generally takes place on the day when trading volume is very heavy and public enthusiasm is near a peak.

A prospective exhaustion gap can develop several days in a row before a reverse in the trend actually developes. Also, remember the introductory words, "After a long and sustained price move."

TIP NO.

#25

DO NOT FALL IN LOVE WITH ANY POSITION

TWENTY-FIVE

Never become attached to or feel content with any market position. Review and question each situation constantly. We live in a competitive world and business conditions are always changing. Re-evaluate the pros and cons of each commitment over and over and over again in order to ensure that no detrimental condition develops unnoticed.

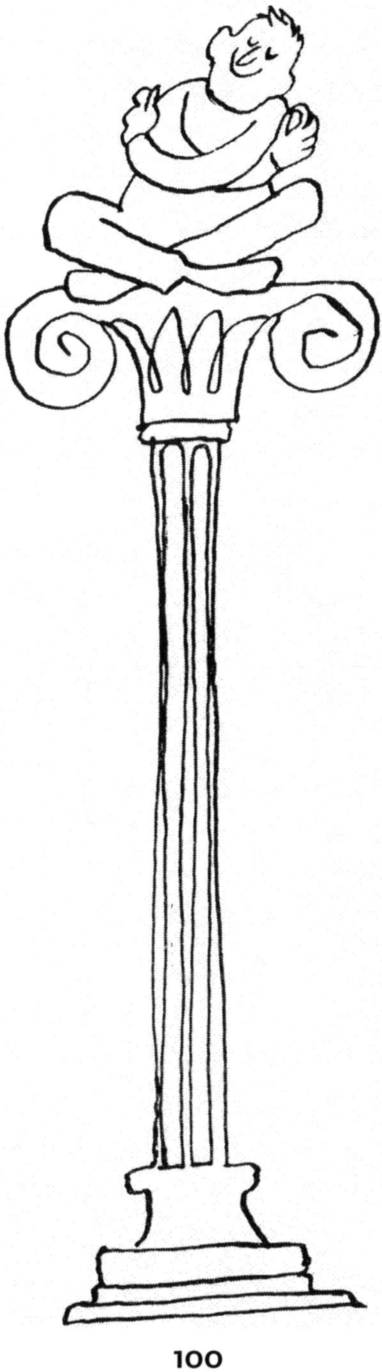

TIP NO.

#26

DO NOT BE A "NAVIGATION HERO"

TWENTY-SIX

Head for port when an entirely new major market situation arises. Changes in legislation or judicial decisions, new record high or low in interest rates, the development of a war, a major terrorist attack. Let others guide the ship through new and uncharted financial waters. Remain a patient observer until the way has been marked and the course is clearly indicated.

Try to confine your trading to those periods when the waters are normal, the wind is positive, and the direction of the current is understandable. Then attempt to maximize mileage from the situation.

TIP NO.

#27

DEVELOP A MARKET PHILOSOPHY OF A SUCCESSFUL MERCHANDISER

TWENTY-SEVEN

A new trader can become both winded and unnerved when 40 or 50 or even 60 % of his trades result in losses. At such times it is important to remember that there is no method by which one can trade successfully without taking many losses. But it will be easier for you to trade and accept these losses if you think of yourself as a merchant dealing in groceries, rather than a financier dealing in securities.

A super market manager's main concern is with the realization of satisfactory monthly, quarterly, or yearly, profit and loss statement. The trader does not dwell daily over the fact that the trader just took a small loss in apples. The trader knows this will be offset by a larger profit in oranges. The trader does not stop buying and selling chickens when competition forces him to cut chickens below his or her cost price. The trader knows this loss will be offset by a larger profit in beef. And the trader does not close the store because conditions suddenly require him to sell Coke at a loss. The trader knows this will be offset by purchases of chips and candy.

To become a successful market trader, try to see yourself as a merchandiser of impersonal stocks, or futures contracts, rather than as a trader of personal bank checks or dollar bills.

TIP NO.

#28

DON'T TRY TO SELL CHRISTMAS TREES ON THE 26TH OF DECEMBER

TWENTY-EIGHT

Be prepared to liquidate your position while there are buyers around that still expect the developments which you originally anticipated when first establishing the position. Do not wait until the time arrives when it is obvious to all that Christmas is over.

It is safe to say that in the future there will be periods of price increases and that there will be periods of price recessions. Financial planning that fails to allow for both risks is in itself an unacceptable risk.

At times, the best way to succeed is to disregard the actions of others and to do the opposite. A successful trader learns to sell while there are still buyers in the marketplace.

BIG
REDUCTIONS

TIP NO.

#29

WHENEVER YOU ARE OUT OF TUNE WITH THE MARKET HEAD FOR THE SIDELINES

TWENTY-NINE

After a trader has established a position, his or her judgment will be challenged by the emotions of hope and fear. Hope that the position will become profitable, or hope that the profit will become larger. Fear that the profit will turn into a loss, or fear that the loss will become greater.

Nothing is more conducive to a fresh perspective than to be out of the market. The sidelines should be considered a rest area where one may retire from the action and observe for a week, two weeks, or for a month. This, until your judgment strengthens with knowledge and confidence—and where energy and enthusiasm can be accumulated for the next challenge.

Whenever hope becomes a greater factor than logic in evaluating a market position, it is usually beneficial to liquidate and stand aside.

10
1

TIP NO.

#30

SCARED MONEY SELDOM COVERS THE COST OF THE TUITION

THIRTY

As you start out on this stimulating venture, you should recognize that there is often a cost for education in speculation. Each of us should be prepared to pay the tuition in the forms of money, time and study.

Unfortunately, the costs cannot be estimated before the journey begins. Each person has their own personality, capacity for and rate of reasoning, as well as manner of interpretation and reaction. Each has different sources of information as well as different financial resources. Each will enter the market at different times.

In addition, every market has its own personality, as does each situation within the market.

Generally speaking, one should not attempt to judge his or her proficiency at speculation until having experienced at least two major up and down cycles in the market.

This can mean two seasons in commodities. It may mean three or four years in the stock market.

Should some of the costs of the tuition become apparent during the initial period of trading, then you are fortunate, for you will develop a respect for the market early in your career.

On the other hand, should early trades be successful, then pyramiding and over-extended commitments often follow. In these cases, respect for the market is often learned later and the cost of tuition is generally greater.

The use of scared money for trading in the early days seldom allows much room for error and the influence of fear psychology usually exacts its penalty. At least at the beginning, until you have some basis for judging your competency at speculation, participation should only be accomplished with excess funds, mad money, or throw away money. But definitely not go-for-broke money, last-ounce-of-blood money, or scared money. As President Truman famously said, "Stay out of the kitchen if you can't stand the heat."

Speculation should not be practiced with funds that are required for life's necessities. To do so, is a poor way to handle one's affairs and such can prove to be a handicap to such a person's market judgment.

The cost of education in the school of speculation can be as much as the cost of a college education, or more. However, the benefits and pleasures derived from successfully learning to trade successfully can be very rewarding.

REVIEW & OBSERVATIONS

You have now acquired a collection of 30 Tips that some traders spend a lifetime trying to determine. Examine and try them over and over again. All will assist you in opening the door to good trading technique.

A few may seem repetitious, but this reflects the similarity for success learned by different traders and then identified by each in a different way. A few may appear to conflict, but as you gain trading experience you will discover that in some market situations there is a very fine-line difference between the application of several rules. Yet as the situation develops further, one will clearly stand out and come to mind and fit the situation.

One very successful trader envisions the initiating of a new trade as that of entering an attractive treasure hall in which there are many doors to many unknown rooms.

The trader first examines each door closely, then listens for the music or the sounds and then decides which one offers the greatest promise. He next opens the door slowly and places his foot in the opening. If everything remains satisfactory the trader continues to make more of a commitment, and finally benefits from the returns the treasure room has to offer.

On the other hand, IF the opening door action encounters the threatening roar of a bear, the trader makes a hasty withdrawal, suffers the slight fright or injury and returns to the reexamination and selection of one of the other doors.

Our laws tell us that to be a successful trader in securities we should select those industries that have favorable business outlooks and then chose outstanding companies with in those industries. These corporations are preliminarily identified by evaluating their rate of sales increase and the ability to convert sales into increased earnings year after year.

Then they should be appraised for the potential of the product and the company to excite public opinion. Nevertheless, no purchase should be made of any security whose current price trend is obviously lower.

Once a commitment has been made in a developing uptrend situation, it should not be liquidated until the price action indicates the price move has been completed (or the position is stopped out).

Charts should be utilized as maps for the price action of each specific commitment in order to easily recognize the beginning and completion of major price movements. Charts should not be read until after the market closes. Buys should be made only if the price is higher than the last two week's high. Sales should be made only if the price is lower than the last two week's low.

When you are considering a commitment, it is important to note whether the daily price bars on a chart are moving upward from the lower left corner to the upper right corner, or moving from the upper left corner downward toward the lower right corner, or only moving sidewise in a neutral channel of congestion.

Stocks or futures which are making initial new highs or lows for the year represent an outstanding prospect list for selecting favorable trading situations.

Above all keep in mind that public psychology, earnings and interest rates are three of the most important "forces" that make the world of stocks and futures prices move up and down.

Markets and price movements are not haphazard affairs. They are governed by certain laws. These include the laws and forces which relate to supply and demand, momentum, probability and action and reaction. There are rules to be identified and used for acting in harmony with these laws.

Education is knowledge, knowledge is wisdom, wisdom is money and money is economic freedom. In America, each of us has the opportunity to acquire as much education, knowledge, wisdom, money and economic freedom as we desire.

(When the above trading rules were first released to the public via the earlier book, The Chicago Tribune presented selected cartoons to its readers on eight consecutive Sundays).

(CONT'D)

AUTHOR BACKGROUND

When Merrill Lynch in the 1950s announced it was starting a campaign to bring Wall Street to all of America, Conrad Leslie quickly joined the firm and became a stockbroker. However, he soon became impatient with the then dormant stock market and felt a greater learning challenge was presented by the daily price activity on the floor at The Chicago Board of Trade.

For many years, Leslie appraised the overnight commodity news and edited preopening market and price chart letters to the brokers of five successive New York Stock Exchange Member Firms, including F.I. DuPont, Thomson McKinnon, Bache & Co., E.F. Hutton and ADM Investors Services. He learned much from observing each stock research department's decisions.

Leslie thought that the USDA first-of-the-month farmer based crop survey estimates, released on the 10th of the month were too delayed to enable efficient buying and selling marketing decisions in Agribusiness. So, he developed and published his own faster issued monthly crop production estimates from card reports received from 1,800 grain elevator managers.

The New York Times identified Conrad Leslie as the most widely read private crop forecaster in the world of Agribusiness. His monthly corn, wheat and soybean statistical production estimates were of such interest to food industry people as to be quickly distributed around the world by Reuters, Dow Jones, and TV and radio news services

Through his first book, daily market analysis to brokers, monthly editorials to 1,800 U.S. grain elevator manager reporters and afternoon Chicago TV market reports, he was persistently among those early few who called on Congress to permit Americans to again own gold.

For decades, the world price of gold was determined once a day in London by a committee of bankers and traders. Leslie was an early promoter for the establishment of an "All Day" gold futures market in Chicago.

American grain export commerce expands with the world's increasing population and its hunger. Price relationships between foreign currencies each day were largely determined via forward pricing contracts at international banks. Again, Leslie was an early advocate for the creation of a "more open" foreign currency futures market in Chicago.

At one time, stock option trades were executed over-the-counter by a few small New York brokers at their determined contract prices. After Leslie received what he considered to be an unethical liquidating sales price, he urged the President of the Chicago Board of Trade, Henry Wilson, to examine the potential for the development at The Board of a futures market for the trading of stock options. Such was created and flourishes.

Additional Information:

Graduated 1947 Miami University with a major in Banking and Finance. First Lt. (retired) U.S. Army Air Force World War ll B-24 Pilot, Thirty-five combat missions over Germany at age 21. Awarded Distinguished Flying Cross and Air Medal with three clusters. Conrad Leslie has now retired.

Photo credit: Thomson Reuters

clesliebooks@gmail.com

30 TIPS FOR BETTER INVESTING

#

Made in United States
Troutdale, OR
11/03/2026

56844508R00075